The SOCCER Alphabet Book

by Stephanie S. Ellis

DEDICATED TO ELLIS VIENNE WHO STARTED ME ON MY SOCCER
JOURNEY

AND TO ALL THOSE YOUNGSTERS WHO PLAY SOCCER
AND TO THE PARENTS AND COACHES WHO ENCOURAGE THEM
IN THEIR SPORT.

All rights reserved. This book, or parts thereof, may not be reproduced
in any form without permission in writing from the publisher.

Copyright, 2015 by Stephanie S. Ellis and Mackenzie Woods Publishing

Library of Congress Cataloging-in-Publication Data
Ellis, Stephanie Shriber,
The soccer alphabet book / Stephanie Shriber Ellis p 47
An overview of alphabetical terms and pictures pertaining to soccer ...

Paperback   ISBN 97809898118 3 5
1. SOCCER ---Educational , Juvenile literature , picture book [1. Soccer] 1.
Title

Published in the United States by Mackenzie Woods Publishing
Printed in USA
First Edition 1

Mackenzie Woods Publishing
www.soccerpals.com

A

ASSISTANT COACH
Helps the coach with the training of the team and carries out a wide variety of duties asked to do by the coach.

AWARDS
Prize for success.

ASSISTANT REFEREE
The linesman who monitors the sidelines to determine if the ball is out of bounds or if players are off sides.

B

BOOTS
An English name for soccer shoes or cleats.

BALL
A sphere shaped ball which is black and white and covered with leather or plastic. A good ball is stitched. 4 - 7 year olds play with a number 3 ball, 8-12 year olds use a number 4 ball and 13 - 18 use a number 5 ball.

BICYCLE KICK
It involves jumping in the air, falling backwards and moving your legs as if to ride a bicycle and kicking the ball over your head. Can be a dangerous kick.

C

CAPTAIN
Player who has been designated by the coach to be the one person who can communicate with the referee. Usually designated by a distinctive arm band.

COACH
The decision maker who decides on plays and lineup while training his team.

CORNER KICK
A kick awarded to the attacking team when the ball is kicked over the end lines by the defending team.

DEFENDERS
A playing position in front of the goal keeper. The players work to prevent goals, by blocking, stealing or any other means.

DRIBBLING
The player moves the ball across the field one small kick at a time, always keeping possession of the ball.

D

E

BALL
JERSEY
SHORTS
SOCKS
SHIN GUARDS
SHOES

EQUIPMENT

FLAG

A flag is used by the linesman to indicate that an infringement to the rules has been made or to indicate substitutions.

FIELD OR PITCH

F

FOUL CARDS

These cards are used by the referee to warn a player or eject a player from the game.

G

GOAL KEEPERS

Each team must have a designated goal keeper. They are the only player on the field who can legally use their hands and only inside of the penalty box. They must wear a different colored uniform from both teams.

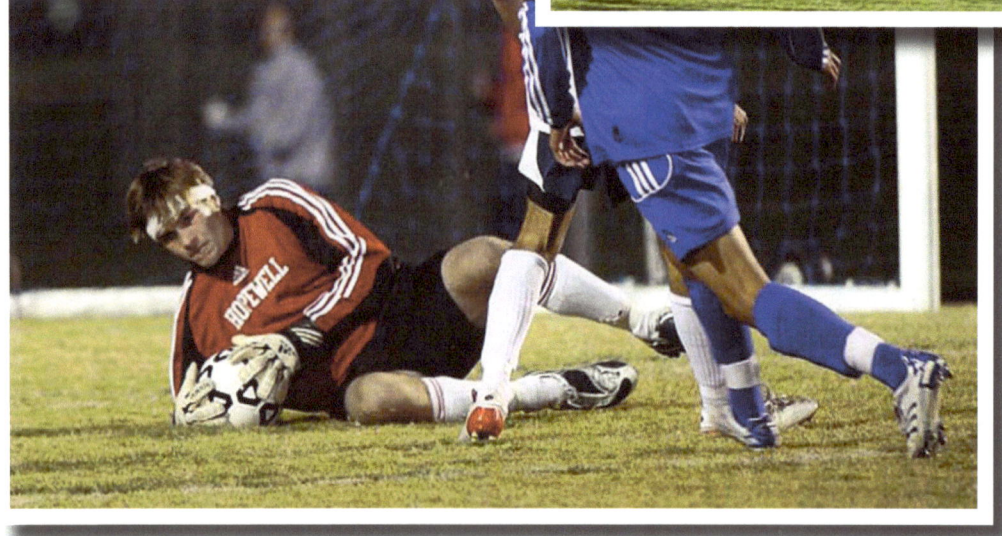

HEADING
Using one's head to pass the ball.

HOLDING
An action by a player against another player; by gripping the opponent and preventing them from moving forward. This action may result in a foul.

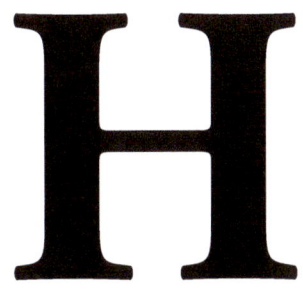

International

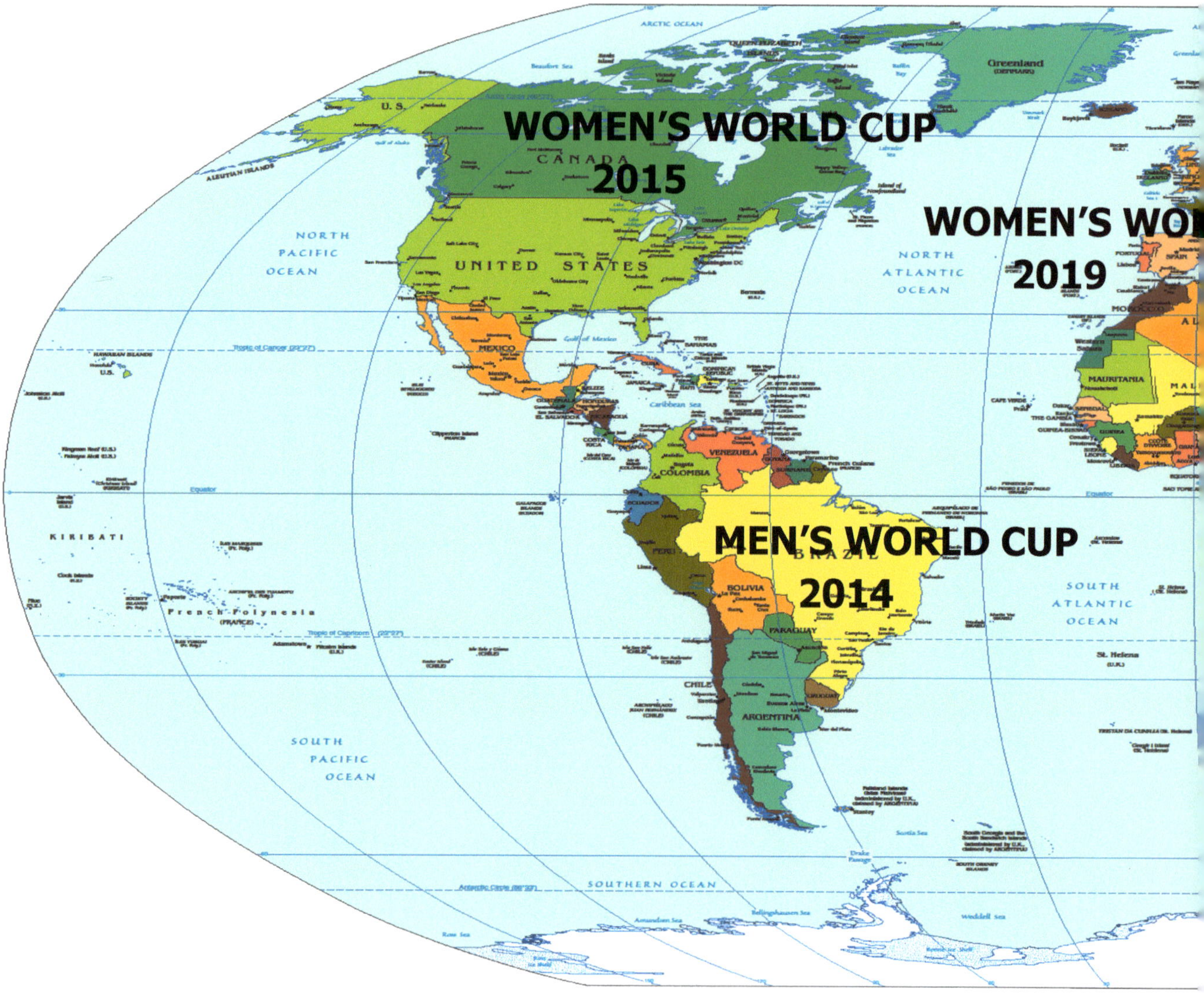

WOMEN'S WORLD CUP 2015

WOMEN'S WORLD CUP 2019

MEN'S WORLD CUP 2014

Soccer

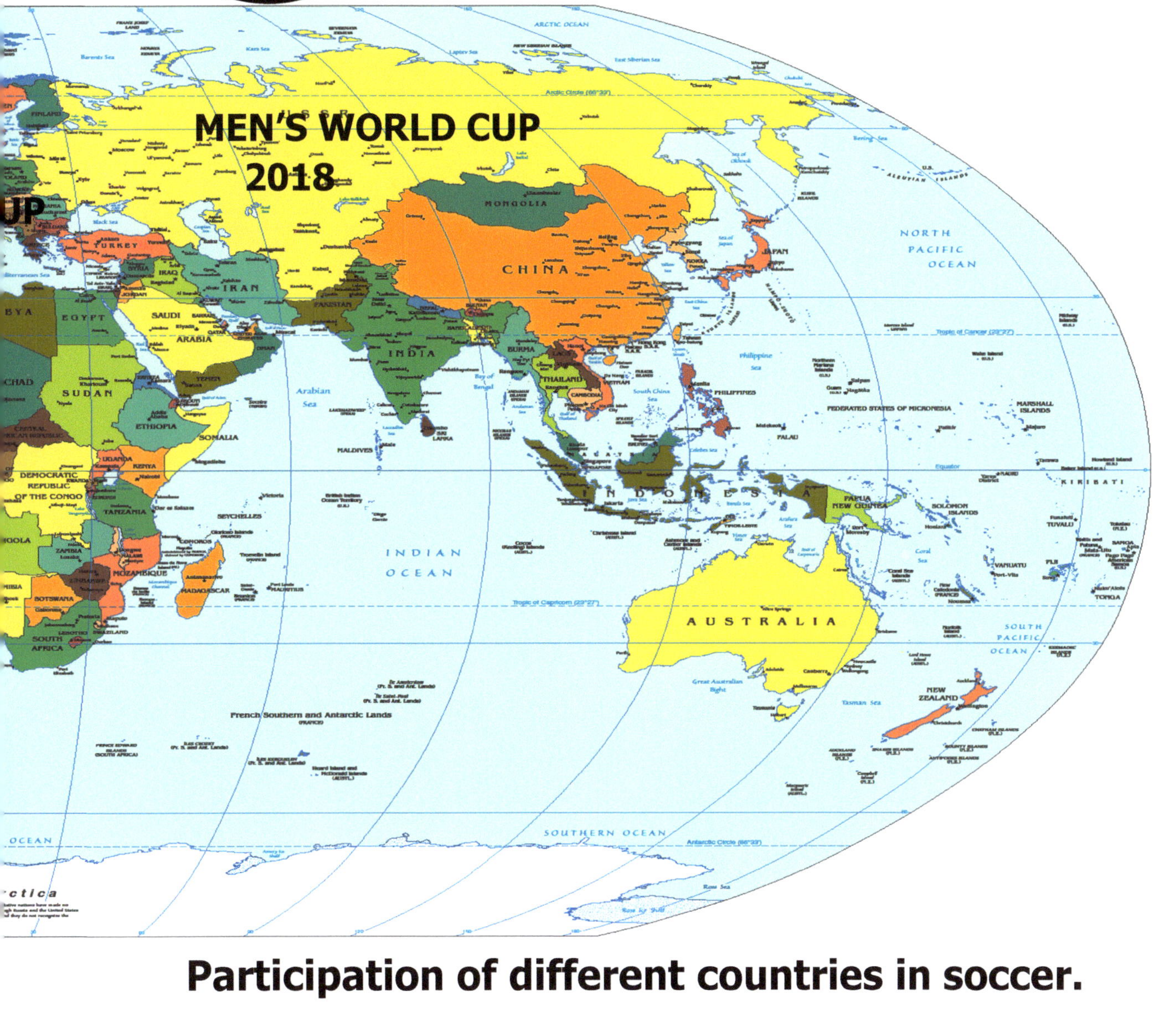

Participation of different countries in soccer.

J

JUGGLING

Juggling requires the player to attempt to keep the ball from touching the ground by bouncing it off his foot, thigh, head or other body parts without using his or her arms or hands.

K

KEEPER

Another word for goal keeper. The final guard for the goal.

SUMMARY OF THE LAWS OF THE GAME

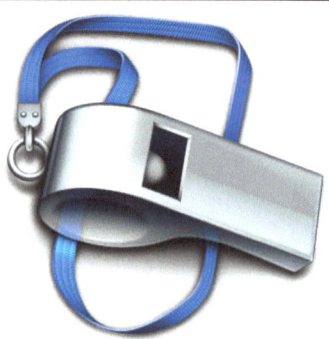

The official soccer rules are called the "Laws of the Game" and are published annually by FIFA. More information and a complete list of the latest rules can be found at www.fifa.com . Rules may be modified for women, players with disabilities and for players under 16 and over 35 years of age. This is a summary of the Laws.

LAW 1. THE FIELD OF PLAY - The field of play is the surface on which the game of soccer is played and is in the shape of a rectangle. This law regulates the line markings and the soccer pitch dimensions which are between 90 and 120 meters long and 45 to 90 meters wide.

LAW 2. THE BALL - The official ball is 26 to 27 inches in circumference and weighs between 410 and 450 grams. Youth teams may play with a smaller ball if they so choose.

LAW 3. NUMBER OF PLAYERS - According to the official soccer rules, a team can bring in ten outfield players and one goal keeper on the pitch with several substitutes on the bench. Youth teams often play with fewer players. [4 vs. 4]

LAW 4. PLAYER'S EQUIPMENT - The rules say that a player must wear a shirt or jersey, footwear, shin pads, shorts and socks and the two teams must have different colors so they can be differentiated on the field. Goal keepers must wear a completely different color from the other field players.

LAW 5. REFEREE - The referee enforces the official rules of soccer. His decisions are final.

LAW 6. LINESMEN - They are assistant referees and help the referee make decisions. One is on each side of the field.

LAW 7. DURATION OF THE MATCH - The official game of soccer is played in two halves, 45 minutes each. This is not the actual time of play, as the clock ticks for injuries and substitutions and time can be added by the referee to balance the clock at the game's end.

LAW 8. THE START OF PLAY- All players must start on their own half of the field. Defending players must be at least ten yards from the ball. The ball must be kicked forward from the center of the field. The ball is "in play" when it has traveled the distance of its own circumference.

LAW 9. BALL IN AND OUT OF PLAY - The ball is considered in play until it has gone completely out of bounds, unless the game is stopped by the referee for another reason.

LAW 10. METHOD OF SCORING - The entire ball must cross the goal line into the goal to score. One point is allowed for a goal. A game may end in a tie.

LAW 11. OFF-SIDE - A player is in an off-side position if the player is closer than the ball is to the opponent's goal line, unless the player is on his or her own side of the field or two opponents are as close to the goal line as the player is.

LAW 12. FOULS AND MISCONDUCT - A foul can occur when the player tries to get the ball from his opponent and kicks him or pushes him away accidentally, whereas misconduct means that a player willfully targets his opponent and punches, kicks or pushes him away. Fouls can only occur while the ball is in play, but misconduct can occur when it's out of play as well. A yellow or red card can be given by the referee.

LAW 13. FREE KICKS - Direct free kick: this kick may be made and a goal scored without the ball first touching another player. Indirect free kick: The goal may not be scored unless the ball touches another player after the kick is made.

LAW 14. PENALTY KICK - A penalty kick is awarded if a foul is committed by a defending player in his or her own penalty area.

LAW 15. THROW-IN - When the ball goes out of play over a sideline, the ball is put back in play with a throw-in. The player must keep both feet on the ground, use both hands, and throw the ball from a position behind the head.

LAW 16. GOAL KICK - When the attacking team plays the ball "out-of bounds" over the goal line, the defending team puts the ball back in play with a goal kick.

LAW 17. CORNER KICK - When the ball is played out-of-bounds over the goal line by the defending team the ball is put back into play by the attacking team with a corner kick.

M

MIDFIELDER

Players in the center of the field who act as attackers.

NET

The net surrounds the end posts and cross bar and is another word for goal. When a ball crosses beneath the cross bar and enters the goal, a point is scored.

NEAR POST

This is the opposite of the far post and is the goal post nearest to the point of attack.

O

OPPONENTS
A team against your team.

OVERHEAD CATCH
The goalie leaps to catch a ball over his head.

PARENT

The family member who sees that we get to practice and to our games. They are crucial to any sports program.

PASSING

The movement of the ball from one player to another player with the use of feet or head.

QUICK START

Often times you will see a player quickly kick the ball and move forward after there has been a delay in the game. If the opponents are not paying attention the player can gain an advantage and momentum with the ball.

REFEREES

The referee is the official of the game and oversees that the rules of the game are applied. The two linesmen assist the center referee with "out of bound" calls, corner kicks, fouls and substitutions. At higher levels of play the referee is assisted by a fourth official who's duties are usually administrative.

RED CARD

If you are shown a red card you are done for the day. It is an ejection notice. It can also come with a suspension of an additional game or more.

R

S STRETCHING

Players warm up their muscles prior to the start of play.

SLIDE TACKLE

When you leave your feet and slide on the ground to win a ball, it shows your opponents who is in charge. But be sure you contact the ball and not the player, or a foul will be called.

TRAPPING

To use the feet, thighs, or chest to get control of the ball and stopping the ball's motion and maneuvering it so a play can be attempted.

T

THROW IN

This refers to putting the ball back into play after it has crossed the sideline. It is the only time a field player can use their hands. The ball must be thrown with both hands, over the head and both feet must be on the ground.

U

UNIFORM

It is the color of the uniform that distinguishes the teams as different. The goalkeepers must have a shirt that distinguishes themselves as different from their team and the opponents.

UNSPORTSMANLIKE BEHAVIOR

A yellow card is a caution and is used to denote unsportsmanlike behavior. A red card is ejection from the game for continual disregard for the rules of the game.

VOLUNTEERS

People who donate their time to help.

VUVUZELAS

Horns which were used in the 2010 World Cup.

V

USA WOMEN WON THE 2015 WORLD CUP

The USA Women's team beat Japan in the finals to win the World Cup in Vancouver in 2015! They played on artificial turf and won $2 million dollars for winning. The 2019 Women's World cup will be held in France.

WORLD CUP

The Men's and Women's World Cups are held every four years in alternating years. For the two years prior many countries compete to qualify to be in the top 32 teams.

In 2014 the World Cup for the men was held in Brazil with Germany becoming the champions. The 2018 Men's World Cup will be held in Russia and then in Qatar in 2022.

THE ROMAN NUMBERAL FOR TEN

There are ten field players on the field plus one goalie for each team.

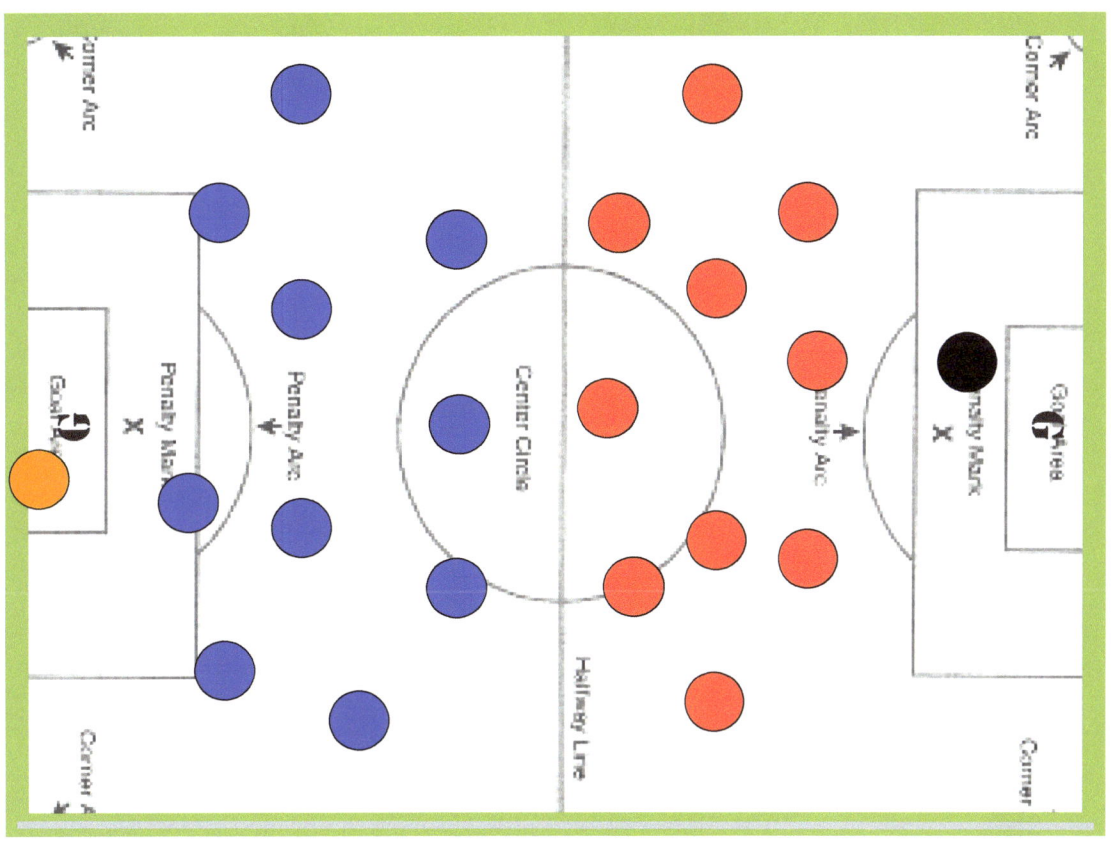

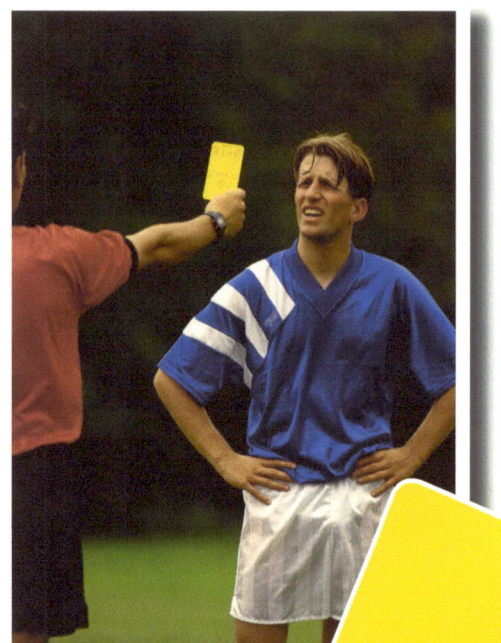

YELLOW CARD

A yellow card is a warning. Usually it is for committing a hard or dangerous foul, arguing with the referee, or using unsportsmanlike language.

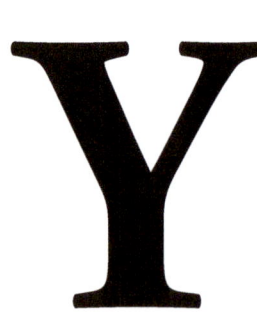

Zero to Zero

Soccer games are usually played in two forty five minute halves. This is different for youth teams and can vary from thirty minute halves to forty minute halves. If the score is zero to zero at the end of the two halves, different scenarios can take place.

The game can be called as a tie, two overtime periods of fifteen minutes each can be played and the first team to score wins, or if the score is still zero to zero at the end of the overtime, five players from each team will have a kick off determining the winner.

GLOSSARY

ASSIST -
Refers to a pass that results in a goal.

ASSISTANT REFEREE -
There are 2 per game, one on each side line, who mainly "call the lines" & offside, but can also report fouls & advise the Referee. On throw-ins, they indicate when the ball is out-of-bounds by pointing the flag in the direction in which the attackers will advance.

ATTACK STALLER -
An attacker who unnecessarily slows down or stalls the attack by making a bad, lazy or selfish decision. Examples include not moving off the ball, holding the ball too long instead of passing it, taking away the opportunity for a fast break by dribbling the ball too long or by passing backwards or sideways instead of forward, and the thoughtless player who too often calls for the ball to be passed backward to him or her when opportunities exist to pass the ball forward.

ADVANTAGE CLAUSE -
A clause in the soccer rules that gives the Referee the discretion to allow play to continue even after a foul has been committed if stopping play would unfairly punish the fouled team.

AGE -
A player's soccer age is usually determined by how old he or she was on the last July 31st.

BACK FOUR -
Often used to describe the defensive line, e.g. right and left back and two central defenders.

BALL -
The spherical object that the game revolves around!

BALL WATCHING -
Describes a soccer player who is not aware of what's going on around them as they are more intent on focusing on the ball rather than players and situations building around them.

BANANA KICK -
Banana Kick Soccer (aka Bending the Ball, Inswinger & Outswinger). A shot kicked into the air that curves like a "banana". The ball curves be

cause of sidespin. If it curves in, it is called an "inswinger"; if out, it is called an "outswinger". This kick is used a lot on corner kicks, to curve into or away from the goal and to curve around defenders, such as to curve around a wall on a free kick.

BLIND SIDE -
Playing the ball to the opposite side of where an opponent is focused.

BLOCK TACKLE -
Strong frontal tackle

BOX - The penalty area / 18 yard box where strikers do the damage.

BREAKAWAY -
Counter attack where rapid movement is made into forward space.

CALLING -
Communication between players.

CAPS –
Every time you play in an International match for your country, you are credited with a "cap".

CHANNELS -
Area approximately 15 yard from the touchline.

CHIP -
Short lofted pass or shot that gets the ball in the air.

CLOSING DOWN -
Players should advance to an opponent with the ball in an attempt to stall play or win back possession.

CLUB -
Teams in all different age brackets belong to Clubs. There are youth teams, amateur teams and so on that belong to dif-

ferent clubs.

COIN TOSS -
A coin is tossed to decide which team will defend or attack during the first or second half.

COMMIT -
Getting the opponent to commit to a course of action so that you can then do the opposite.

CONTROL - Bringing the ball under control by cushioning its arrival with a surface on the body. Also can refer to possession and tempo of the play as the key to having control of the soccer game.

CORNER FLAG -
Markers that determine the boundary of the playing field. They are used to determine whether the ball has crossed the sideline or the goal line.

CORNER KICK -
A corner kick is a method of restarting play. When the ball goes out of bounds over the end line (aka the "Goal Line") and was last touched by the defending team, the attacking team inbounds it from the nearest corner by kicking it in from the corner.

COVER -
Defensively where a second soccer player provides cover to another player.

CROSS -
A long pass often in the air that is played diagonally from the flanks or channels across the field or into the box.

CROSS BAR -
The bar which runs at the top of the goal.

DECOY RUN -
Where a soccer player executes a run to draw attention from the intended play. Also known as creating space.

DEFENDERS -
Players who should stop, hold up and minimize any attempts on goal.

DRIBBLE -
The art of close control while

moving with the soccer ball at the feet. Any time you have a pass, take it. Dribble only when you can't pass or if you can dribble & score.

DUMMY -
Similar to decoy, any trick, technique or skill that unbalances or confuses an opponent and can send them the wrong way in order to gain an advantage.

EARLY BALL - Simple phase of soccer play where an immediate pass is played to a team mate at the earliest opportunity, often to exploit space.

ENDURANCE -
Power to last or keep on.

ENERGY -
Active strength or healthy power.

EFFORT –
Exertion of power, physical or mental.

EXERCISE –
Active use that gives practice or training or causes improvement.

EXTRA TIME –
Time added on by the referee to make up time lost in delays of the game.

FAKEOVER -
Technique where a player looks as if they are to take the ball from their team mate who is in possession but they don't and just run past each other.

FEINT -
An action that attempts to confuse and trick an opponent e.g. step over, scissors, Beardsley,
Ronaldhino, Cryff Ronaldo, All have feints named after them.

FIFA –
Founded in 1904 to establish soccer's official rules and provide unity among national soccer associations. They sponsor the WORLD CUP and oversee Olympic Soccer competition. They are located in Zurich, Switzerland.

FIELD –

The rectangular area surrounded by boundary lines, making up the area of play, sometimes referred to as the pitch.

FIRST TOUCH -
Vital skill of any soccer player is to be able to get the ball under control and set up their next option, often known as their first touch.

FLANK -
The 10 - 15 yards from the side lines, often where crosses come in from.

FLIGHT -
Referred to the flight of the soccer ball.

FORWARD –
Offensive player who plays closest to the opponents goal. Their main purpose is to score or help a teammate to score.

FOUL –
Any play that is breaking the rules. A foul can result in a free kick, or a
direct or indirect kick, depending upon the foul.

FREE KICK -
A kick that is awarded to a team that has been fouled by the opposition or a dead ball restart situation when play has been stopped by the referee for an infringement of the laws of the game.

GIVE AND GO -
Where a player passes the ball and then moves to receive the ball back from the player they played it to... also known as wall pass or 1 - 2.

GOAL -
Something every team needs to focus on, whether it Is defending or scoring!

GOAL SIDE -
The area between ball and the goal when defending.

HANDBALL -
An offense where the player is seen to intentionally use his or her hand or arm to play the ball. If the goalkeeper uses his hands outside the penalty box it is a foul.

HALFTIME -
A break or interval taken between the two halves usually fifteen minutes.

HALF VOLLEY - when a player volleys (using their laces) an upward bouncing ball that has just landed in front of them.

HAT TRICK -
This is three goals scored by the same player in one game.

HEADING -
Using the head to direct the balls flight.

HEEL PASS - Striking the ball with the heel to kick it backward, rather than forward. Usually used as a surprise move to avoid a tackle.

HIGH KICK - dangerously kicking.

HIGH PRESS -
Tactical deployment of the soccer team where all players apply immediate pressure to the opponents when possession is conceded, often in opponents half.

HOLLYWOOD BALL -
An ambitious pass that is only seen in the movies!

INSTEP -
Upper surface of the foot, when coaching players it's the laces part of the boot!

INSWINGER - where the flight of the ball arcs towards the target jockeying - delaying and holding up play, not diving in with a tackle but staying up right and preventing the advancement of the opponent.

KILLER PASS -
A perfectly timed and weighted pass through a defense on to the foot of a team mate.

LATE TACKLE -
An unfair challenge, where a soccer player commits a tackle after an opponent has already played the ball.

LINE (HOLDING THE) -
Defensive term where the defenders keep an imaginary line to catch opponents offside.

LINE OF RECOVERY -
When a player is beaten, this is the line on which they retreat back towards their own goal to get goal side of the attack.

LOFTED PASS -
A high pass executed by kicking the bottom half of the ball sending it into the air.

MAN TO MAN MARKING -
A system that can be deployed where individuals are given specific tasks of marking individuals.

MARK A MAN -
Is to move with the player you are guarding and to stay with him wherever he goes on the field to prevent the player from receiving the ball.

MENTAL DISCIPLINE –
Keeping your mind in the game

MENTAL GAME -
High concentration.

MIDFIELDER BOOT -
A long high kick from midfield.

MUSCLE –
A bundle of special tissue which can be tightened or loosen to move parts of the body.

NARROWING THE ANGLE -
Closing down a player so that the angle they have to shoot or pass is reduced significantly.

ODP –
The Olympic Development Program was developed to help discover elite players to build the National team pool.

OFFSIDES -
A tricky rule to understand. The situation where an attacking player, on the offensive half of the field, has put himself in a position where there are fewer than two opponents between him and the goal. The goalkeeper counts as one of the opponent. This positioning does not constitute a foul, until he becomes involved in the play.

OFF THE BALL -
Movement of players, to create space and provide options.

OFFSIDE TRAP -
When a defender(s) acting on a common understanding or moves forward in a line to catch one or more opponents offside.

ONE TOUCH -
Players move the ball quickly and immediately when they receive it.

OUT OF BOUNDS -
When the ball crosses the touchlines or the lines at the end of the field.

OUTSWINGER -
When a ball is played but curls away from the target.

OWN GOAL -
When the ball goes off of an opponent into his own goal, a goal is scored for the opposite team.

OVERTIME -
Time added by the referee.

PENALTY KICK -
A free kick is given when a foul occurs in the penalty box.

PITCH -
The area surrounded by boundary lines, making up the area of play.

PROFESSIONAL -
A player who is paid.

PUNT -
The kick that is made by the goalkeepers down field by kicking the ball high in the air towards the opponents' goal.

RECEIVING -
Technique required to control an incoming ball.

RUNNING WITH THE BALL -
Player in possession exploits space by carrying the ball quickly and efficiently; different from dribbling as a player must beat an opponent.

SAVE –
A term used to describe when the goalkeeper prevents the ball from entering the goal.

SCISSOR KICK -
Scissors Kick is also another name for "Bicycle Kick".

SCOUTS -
Quite often volunteers that watch local junior and youth soccer for professional clubs to eye the talent and recommend them for academy trials.

SERVICE -
Used to describe whether or not the attackers / strikers as getting quality balls played into them e.g. "attackers are just not getting the service!"

SHADOW PLAY -
Playing without opponents.

SHIELDING -
Keeping possession and control of the ball by using the body to come between the ball and the opponent.

SHOT ON GOAL - a shot that hits the goal frame or is blocked by the goal keeper.

SHOW -
When a player makes himself available.

SLIDING TACKLE -
When a defending player goes to ground and uses an extended leg to win the ball.

SPACE -
Creating, exploiting and running into space.

SQUARE BALL -
A ball that is played from one side of the pitch to another, laterally.

STARTER -
The original eleven players who begin the game.

STOPPER -
A center fullback or a player who plays between the FB's & MF'S who is good at stopping attacks up the center.

STRETCHING THE PLAY -
Making the pitch big, wide and deep.

STRIKER -
A scoring forward, usually a center forward who is very skilled at scoring.

SUBSTITUTION-
A new player replaces a player

who has been playing in the game.

SUDDEN DEATH -
When a game is tied, sudden death is a term used to describe how the continued play happens. It means that the first team to score wins.

SUPPORT PLAY -
Team mates move into and create space and options for the player in possession.

SWEEPER -
A fast & tough player who usually plays just behind the full backs, although he is allowed to roam. His job is to cover the space between the fullbacks & the goal keeper & to stop any balls giving the defense time to recover.

SWITCHING PLAY -
Changing the angle of attack.

TACKLE -
To use the feet or shoulder to take the ball away from a member of the opposing team. A challenge to win the ball.

TAKING A PLAYER ON -
When a player in possession runs at a defending player with the aim of going past them.

TARGET MAN -
A striker / attacker (often big and shields the ball well) who should always be available for a pass from the midfield who can then hold up the play until reinforcements arrive.

TEAM MANAGER -
The person who helps the coach and keeps records for the team.

THIRDS -
The pitch can be segmented roughly into a defensive, a midfield and attacking third all of which are approximately 35 yards (give or take a couple)

THROUGH PASS -
A pass which is played between two defenders for an attacker to run onto.

TIE – A tied game is equal scores on both sides.

TIME OUT –
The referee may call time out when he feels that it is necessary.

TOUCHLINE -
Also known as the sidelines. The lines are included as part of the field of play.

TRAVEL TEAM -
Serious youth junior soccer where teams regularly play out of state games.

TRIALS -
Term used to describe a process of evaluation on a players ability and suitability for a team.

TURNING AN OPPONENT
When running at an opponent, the use of feints and fakes to trick the opponent into turning or by pushing the ball past them and causing them to turn.

UNITED STATES YOUTH SOCCER - **USYSA** United States Youth Soccer Association, a branch of the USSF.

UNSPORTING BEHAVIOR -
The Referee can give a Yellow Card for behavior which in the Referee's judgment is unsporting or causes an unfair advantage. If a player on the college level receives five yellow cards during the season he must sit out the next game.

VICTORY -Success or winning.

VISUALIZATION -
Seeing in your mind.

VOLLEY -
A ball is kicked in the air before it touches the ground. If kicked in front with the "laces", it is called a "volley"or "instep volley"; if the ball is to one side it is called a "side volley"; if the inside of the foot is used it is an "inside-of-foot volley" (this might be used close to goal or for a short pass). A player should lock his ankle when volleying so the foot is firm. On a front volley, proper technique is to bring the foot to the height of the ball by raising the knee (so the portion of the leg between the knee & the ankle is vertical); the technique is

44

different from a regular kick.

WALL -
At U-8 & older, when the other soccer team has a "free kick", players may stand side-by-side between the ball & their goal so they form a "wall". Then the kicker doesn't have a direct attack on goal from a dead ball situation. They will have to stand the required distance back.

WARMUP EXERCISES -
At age 10 and older, children become susceptible to muscle pulls. When you move up to U-11, you should have your team warm up their muscles before playing. You should have them warm up their muscles by light activities such as jogging or slowly dribbling a ball around the field. The light warm up is important because it "warms up" the muscles which makes them stretch easier & less likely to tear.

WEAK SIDE -
The side of the field where the players have moved away from.

WEIGHT OF THE PASS -
Key ingredient to a perfect pass, the pace or power of the kick.

WIDE PLAYERS -
Often called wingers who play near the touch line.

WHISTLE -
Instrument used by the referee to stop play by blowing a shrill sound.

WORK RATE -
Players and teams contribution to the game.

WRONG SIDE -
When an opponent is allowed to get between the defender and the goal.

ZONAL MARKING -
A system where players have a specific area that they have to cover.

45

Other books written by Stephanie S. Ellis

MY PERSONAL SOCCER JOURNAL

An Educational Guide and record keeping journal for all children who play soccer. It is a fun and informative text starting when they begin their journey whether they are four, six, eight or twelve years old. It covers the history and different levels of soccer while giving both the children and the parents an introduction to the adventures ahead of them.

The BASEBALL Alphabet Book

The BASEBALL Alphabet book [like The SOCCER Alphabet Book] is a picture book for children from six to twelve years of age using the 26 letters of the alphabet and pictures to describe over 100 baseball terms and definitions. The pictures tell a story and help the children to understand baseball terms. It is a fun and educational book for all parents and children who love the game of baseball.

Stephanie Shriber Ellis always wanted to work with children, was graduated from the University of Akron and started her career as an early Elementary school teacher in Erie, Pennsylvania. She founded the first private licensed Nursery School in the State.

Following her grandson while he participated in various youth athletics, she saw the need to help children understand the terms of the different sports and become more self confident as they played in the numerous activities.

Her books are fun, informative and educational tools for children from six to twelve years of age and give a good understanding of each sport in pictures and words. She lives in Florida with her family, two dogs and three feisty cats.

Visit us at:
www.soccerpals.com
www.mackenziewoodspublishing.com

www.ingramcontent.com/pod-product-compliance
Lightning Source LLC
Chambersburg PA
CBHW041535040426
42446CB00002B/96